Success in Science
Test Booster

Alan McMurdo
Ruth Wylie
Series Editor: Jayne de Courcy

AGES 10–11

Contents

Collins Educational
An Imprint of HarperCollinsPublishers

The ⭐3 Steps to Success ...

Step 1

Complete Test practice papers

⭐ *Success in Science: Test Booster* **gives your child the opportunity to practise answering Test papers A and B that are set in the Science National Test at the end of Key Stage 2. Both Test papers span a range of Science topics.**

⭐ **All the questions are either taken from National Test papers or are Test-style questions. You can use the book to give 'Test practice', to check on the level at which your child is currently performing, or to diagnose difficulties.**

Step 2

Detailed answers and guidance

⭐ **The authors, who are KS2 Test Markers, have identified the best answer to each question. Other answers which would be awarded marks, but which are not as scientifically accurate, are also shown in the 'Answer' box.**

⭐ **The detailed guidance in 'How to tackle the question' allows you to help your child work through a question which has caused difficulty. It explains the wording of the question and also the Science needed to answer it.**

Step 3

Extra revision

⭐ **In the *Answers and Guidance*, the 'Inside the Science' box provides a description of the Science knowledge and skills needed to answer each question. This will help you to identify the areas of Science which may be causing your child difficulty.**

⭐ **References are also given to the chapters in *Success in Science Books 1–4* where the relevant aspects of the Science needed are covered in a clear, child-friendly manner.**

⭐ **In this way, you can diagnose where your child may be having difficulty and find appropriate help quickly and easily. <u>No other Test practice book provides this amount of cross-referencing and support</u>. It will help your child improve his or her performance in the KS2 Science National Test.**

Helping your child

⭐ **Don't set your child both papers on the same day. In the Science National Test they will be on different days.**

⭐ **In the Science National Test, 35 minutes is allowed for each paper. At home, tell your child that they have 35 minutes to complete the paper. Then time how long it actually takes them. If your child is working accurately but slowly, they need practice in answering questions faster.** *Success in Science Books 1–4* **have lots of timed practice questions.**

⭐ **The pencil symbol shows where to write each answer. If your child finds reading difficult, you may read the test to them using only the words that are given. This is allowed in the actual Test.**

⭐ **Encourage your child to spend time reading each question carefully. Mistakes are often made by children misreading the questions or rushing in without thinking about their answer.**

Marks and levels

⭐ **Once your child has completed both papers, you can add up their marks and work out the level they would probably be awarded.**

⭐ **For the two papers contained in this book, 21–41 marks would gain a level 3, 42–62 marks would gain a level 4 and 63 marks and above would gain a level 5.**

Note to teachers

⭐ **This book, and the other four titles in the** *Success in Science* **series, are designed for use at home and in school in Years 5 and 6.**

⭐ **The** *Test Booster* **will provide invaluable Test practice for children in Year 6 who are approaching their Science National Test at the end of Key Stage 2. It will support teachers in identifying the 'best' answers to questions: those which are scientifically most accurate and therefore 'safest' in achieving marks.**

⭐ **It will also provide diagnostic support to teachers by identifying areas of scientific weakness. Using the cross-referenced material in** *Success in Science Books 1–4* **will help raise children's performance in their Science National Test.**

1

Plants

(a) The parts of this plant have been labelled.

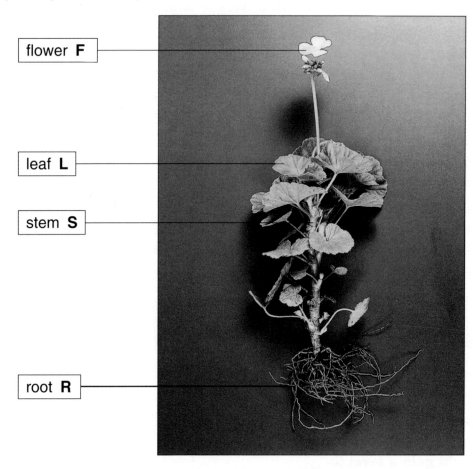

flower **F**

leaf **L**

stem **S**

root **R**

Which part of the plant does each of the following jobs?

Write a letter for the correct part of the plant in the box.

(i) Part of the plant which anchors the plant in the soil

1 mark

(ii) Part of the plant where pollination takes place

1 mark

(b) Which of these describes a plant?

Tick **ONE** box.

consumer ☐   prey ☐

predator ☐   producer

1 mark

2 Materials around the Home

(a) Conner and Dave discussed the materials some things were made from and the reasons why they were used.

Complete the statements below by writing **ONE** correct letter in each box.

Use a letter only once.

A – an electrical insulator	B – transparent	C – strong

D – waterproof	E – an electrical conductor

 (i)   Wood is used for the shelf because it is ☐

1 mark

(ii) Glass is used for the fish tank because it is ☐

1 mark

(iii) Plastic is used for the outside of the electrical cable because it is ☐

1 mark

(b) Ruth investigated the properties of some materials she had found around her home.

She recorded her results in a table.

Complete the table.

One row has been done for you.

Materials	Properties			
	conducts electricity	waterproof	transparent	magnetic
paper tissue	....	....	....	....
wine glass	....	....	....	....
steel drawing pin	yes	yes	no	yes
gold earring	....	....	....	....

1 mark

1 mark

1 mark

3 **Sound**

(a) Anna plays the violin.

As well as using a bow, Anna can also pluck or twang the strings with her finger to play a note.

What is happening to the violin string when it is making a sound?

....

1 mark

(b) Anna can change the force with which she twangs the string. She can pluck hard or more gently to change the loudness of the note.

Describe how the loudness of the sound is affected by the force of Anna's pluck on the string.

....

....

2 marks

(c) Anna turns the screw at the top of the violin to loosen the string, making it less tight.

> What effect does this have on the pitch of the sound the string makes when Anna plucks it?

✏ ....

1 mark

(d) The children in the school listen to Anna play the violin in assembly.

> What does the sound from the violin travel through to get to the children's ears?

✏ ....

1 mark

4

Ice Lollies

(a) Rachel and Tim decided to investigate to find out which teacher had the coldest classroom. Mrs Saxton's remark about her classroom gave them an idea.

My room is really chilly!

Well, mine is so cold that even an ice lolly wouldn't melt in there!

They used four ice lollies from the school kitchen.

The lollies were the same size and shape.

They put one lolly in a bowl in each classroom.

They measured the time taken for each ice lolly to melt completely.

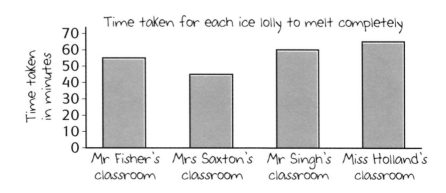

Time taken for each ice lolly to melt completely

7

Look at the bar chart.

Which classroom was the coldest?

✎ ....

1 mark

(b) Describe how the temperature of the classroom affects the time taken for the ice lolly to melt.

✎ ....

....

2 marks

5 **Circuits**

(a) The children make a working model of a lighthouse.

foil   paperclip

Wire

The switch in the circuit is made of card and aluminium foil.

In the picture, the switch is open.

What will happen to the bulb when the switch is closed?

✎ ....

1 mark

(b) Explain why this will happen when the switch is closed.

✎ ....

....

1 mark

8

(c) Their circuit has one battery, one bulb and one switch.

> Draw a circuit diagram to show their circuit.

Use only these symbols.

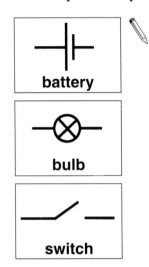

(d) The children want the bulb to glow more brightly.

They use new batteries.

> In which of the circuits below would the bulb glow most
> brightly when the switch is closed?

 Tick **ONE** box.

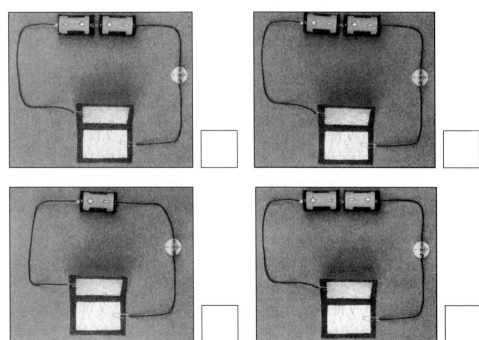

1 mark

6   **Woodlice**

(a) The children decided to find out which conditions woodlice prefer.

They prepared a box which gave woodlice a choice of four different sections labelled **A**, **B**, **C** and **D**.

They carried out a fair test.

They placed 20 woodlice in the centre of the box.

The woodlice could move around easily.

Plan of box, showing conditions

A	B
dry soil	dry soil
plenty of light	no light
C	**D**
damp soil	damp soil
plenty of light	no light

After 20 minutes the children counted how many woodlice were in each section.

They did the investigation two more times.

> Why did they carry out their investigation three times?

....

....

1 mark

(b) They recorded their results in a table.

	Number of woodlice in the different sections			
	A	B	C	D
First time	1	1	5	13
Second time	2	2	5	11
Third time	2	0	4	14

Look at the information in the table.

Which conditions do woodlice prefer?

✎ ....

1 mark

(c) The children wanted to find some more woodlice.

In which of these habitats would they be **most likely** to find woodlice?

Tick **TWO** boxes.

✎ on a playground ☐   under a rotting log ☐

on a flower ☐   in the sea ☐

1 mark

under a stone ☐   on sandy soil ☐

1 mark

(d) Shrews eat woodlice.
Woodlice eat rotting leaves.

— **shrew**

Complete the food chain for woodlice, leaves and shrews.

✎ .... ➜ .... ➜ ....

1 mark

7   **Scales**

(a) These scales measure in newtons.

They work because the spring inside is compressed when an object is placed in the pan.

100N   10N
90N   20N
80N   30N
70N   40N
60N   50N

Complete the sentence.

The newton is the unit used to measure ....

1 mark

(b) Kerry and Jason adjust the scales to zero before weighing an object.

What is the weight of the object in the picture on page 11?

.... N

1 mark

(c) Jason pushes down on the scales.

The pan pushes up on his hand.

What is causing the pan to push up on his hand?

....

....

1 mark

(d) The teacher asked the children to turn the scales sideways and adjust the scales to zero.

Jason pushes on the top of the scales and Kerry pushes on the base.

They hold the scales still.

Jason's push measures 80N.

What is the size of Kerry's push?

....

1 mark

8

Temperature Sensor

(a) Tina is using a temperature sensor and computer to measure some temperatures.

The sensor is made of metal.

> Why is metal a good material to use for the temperature sensor rod?

Tick **ONE** box.

magnetic material ☐   good thermal conductor ☐

shiny ☐   melts ☐

bends easily ☐

1 mark

(b) The children measured the temperature of the air in the room. Next, Robert gripped the sensor with both hands, held it for a short time and then let it go.

The screen showed their results.

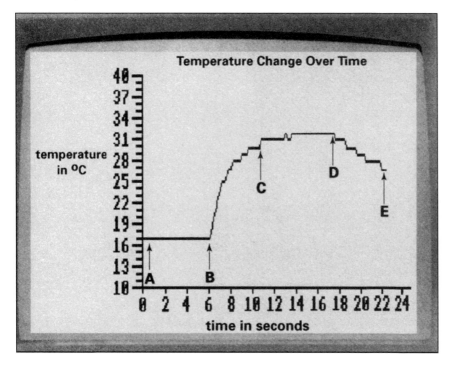

Look at the graph shown on the screen.

What was the temperature of the air in the room?

✎ .... °C

1 mark

(c) Which letter on the screen shows when Robert first gripped the sensor?

Tick **ONE** box.

A ☐   B ☐   C ☐   D ☐   E ☐

1 mark

(d) Which letter shows when Robert removed his hands?

Tick **ONE** box.

A ☐   B ☐   C ☐   D ☐   E ☐

1 mark

(e) Describe what happened to the **temperature** between points **D** and **E**.

✎ ....

1 mark

9

Life Cycle of an Apple Tree

(a) Satjit and Ravi have been finding out about the life cycle of an apple tree. They decide to make a book to show the stages of the life cycle in the right order.

The stages they want to include are:

A pollination	**D** seed dispersal
B fruit production	**E** growing tree
C germination	**F** flower production

Put the letter showing each stage in the correct order on each page of the book.

Three pages have been done for you.

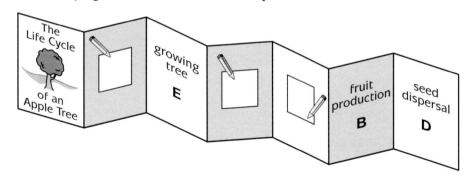

1 mark

1 mark

1 mark

(b) Apple trees are pollinated by insects.

What does the insect carry from one flower to another?

....

1 mark

(c) Some plants use the wind to help with pollination. The wind is also useful for some plants to help them in another part of their life cycle.

What does the wind help many plants do?

....

1 mark

Answers and Guidance

Test A

A1 Plants

Answer

a) i)	R	*1 mark*
ii)	F	*1 mark*

How to tackle the question

 An easy question to start the test. For part (a), the plant root holds the plant in the ground and pollination takes place in the flower. Remember, pollination happens when pollen is transferred to the stigma of a flower.

Inside the Science

 This part of the question is testing your knowledge of the jobs of each part of the plant.
See *Collins Success in Science Book 3*, Chapters 1 and 2

Answer

b) producer ✔		*1 mark*

How to tackle the question

 For part (b), the plant is able to make its own food using water and air and energy from the Sun. In a food chain we call the plant that starts the chain the producer. The other terms, consumer, prey and predator, are other parts of the food chain that come later. They are not used to describe plants.

 You were told to write a letter for part (a) and put a tick in part (b). Do not risk doing anything else!

Inside the Science

 This part of the question is about food chains.
See *Collins Success in Science Book 4*, Chapter 2

A2 Materials around the Home

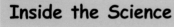

Answer

a) i)	C	*1 mark*
ii)	B (or D)	*1 mark*
iii)	A (or D)	*1 mark*
You may only use D once.		

How to tackle the question

 This question asks you to match each material to one of its properties that is needed for the material to be good at its job. One reason wood is used for shelves is that it is strong. Glass is good for fish tanks because it is transparent and waterproof (either answer could get you a mark). The tricky thing is to make sure you say plastic is good for a cable covering because it is an electrical insulator, not a conductor. A common mistake is for children to just see the word 'electrical' and tick the wrong box.

 If you read the question carefully this should be an easy one to answer. You were told to write one correct letter in each box and use a letter only once. Once you have used D you cannot use it again.

 If you write in the correct word, rather than the letter, you will still get the mark but try to follow the instructions in the question. This will save you time and increase your chances of getting the mark.

Inside the Science

 This part of the question is about the properties of materials and how they are used.
See *Collins Success in Science Book 2*, Chapter 1

Question A2 continued...

Answer

b)

Materials	Properties				
	conducts electricity	waterproof	transparent	magnetic	
paper tissue	no	no	no	no	*1 mark*
wine glass	no	yes	yes	no	*1 mark*
steel drawing pin	yes	yes	no	yes	
gold earring	yes	yes	no	no	*1 mark*

Inside the Science

 This part of the question is also about properties but it goes a bit further and asks about magnetism and electrical conductors.

See *Collins Success in Science Book 2*, Chapters 1 and 2

How to tackle the question

 To answer this question you need to know what each of the properties in the heading of the table means. If something conducts electricity it means that electricity can flow through it, and you could make it into part of a circuit. Metals conduct electricity very well so the steel drawing pin and the gold earring are the two conductors in this table.

 If an object is waterproof, it will not let water through it. The water would run off the side instead. Paper tissue goes soggy when water is poured on it; it definitely is not waterproof! All the other objects are waterproof.

 If an object is transparent you can see through it because it lets light pass through it. You can only see through the wine glass in the table.

 If something is magnetic it means it will be attracted to a magnet. The only magnetic material in this list is the steel drawing pin. A common mistake is for children to think that all metals are magnetic, but only iron, steel, nickel and cobalt are magnetic.

 The question showed you how to fill in the table using the words 'yes' and 'no' by giving you an example, with the steel drawing pin results. You would still get the marks if you used ticks for 'yes' and crosses for 'no'.

A3 Sound

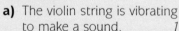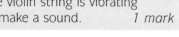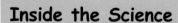

Answer

a) The violin string is vibrating to make a sound. *1 mark*

Inside the Science

 This part of the question is about objects vibrating to make a sound.

See *Collins Success in Science Book 2*, Chapter 5

How to tackle the question

 The important word to use here is vibrate. Remember, things vibrate to make a noise. Always try and be as clear as you can and use the scientific word if you can remember it. A common mistake that children make is to say the string moved. They do not say how the string moves and so their answer does not give enough detail. 'The string moved up and down' or 'the string made the air vibrate' would both get the mark.

 You also need to make sure you answer the question. For example, 'it made sound waves' is a true statement but it does not answer the question and say what the violin string is doing to make the sound.

Answers and Guidance

Answer

b) The **bigger** the force of Anna's pluck on the string the **louder** the sound.   *2 marks*

How to tackle the question

In questions like this you have to describe a pattern and make a link between two things (these are called variables). Here you are asked to link the loudness of the sound and the size of force of Anna's pluck on the string. The answers that get the 2 marks describe the trend or change that applies to all the results. For example, 'the bigger the pluck the louder the sound', or 'the harder the twang the louder the sound', or 'the softer the pluck the quieter the sound', would also get 2 marks.

You would score 1 mark if you wrote about one or two results in the pattern. For example, if you write, 'the loudest sound is made by the biggest force plucking the string', you have described only one result. If you write, 'the biggest force was loudest and the smallest was quietest', you have described two separate results but not linked them.

Inside the Science

This part of the question is about the loudness of sound and also about describing patterns in results. This type of test question is covered in great detail throughout the series of *Success in Science*, in particular in Book 4, Chapter 6.

See *Collins Success in Science Book 2, Chapter 5*, about sound, and *Collins Success in Science Book 4, Chapter 6*, about patterns in results

How to tackle the question

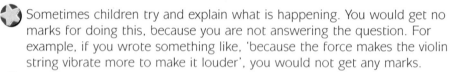
Sometimes children try and explain what is happening. You would get no marks for doing this, because you are not answering the question. For example, if you wrote something like, 'because the force makes the violin string vibrate more to make it louder', you would not get any marks.

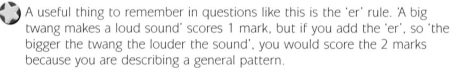
A useful thing to remember in questions like this is the 'er' rule. 'A big twang makes a loud sound' scores 1 mark, but if you add the 'er', so 'the bigger the twang the louder the sound', you would score the 2 marks because you are describing a general pattern.

Finally, in questions like this, make sure you use the variables you are asked about. In this question you are asked about loudness and size of Anna's pluck on the string. Why throw marks away by writing about anything else?

Answer

c) If the violin string is less tight the sound gets lower   *1 mark*

Inside the Science

This part of the question is about the pitch of sound.

See *Collins Success in Science Book 2, Chapter 5*

How to tackle the question

A violin string behaves like an elastic band when it is twanged. If a band is tight or a string is tight the sound will be high. If you loosen the elastic band or string so that it is not so stretched, it will twang to make a much lower sound. It might help to remember **Lo**oser ➔ **Lo**wer. 'The sound (or tone) goes down (or gets deeper or flatter)' would also get the mark.

The most common mistake children make is to give an answer that can be confused with loudness. For example, 'it goes softer' gets no marks (softer means quieter not lower). Sometimes children write too much about the pitch changing and the loudness changing. They get the first part right, but then lose the mark because they have used some wrong science. Make sure you read the question and answer it as clearly as you can. You do not need to write a lot.

Question A3 continued...

Answer

d) Sound travels through air *1 mark*

Inside the Science

 This part of the question is about sound travelling through air.

See *Collins Success in Science Book 2,* Chapter 5

How to tackle the question

Sound can travel through all sorts of materials. To reach your ears, the sound has to travel through the air. Make sure your answer is clear and keep it simple. If you use words like 'vibrations', 'sound waves' or 'ear drum', you are on the right lines, giving good information, but it is not answering the question so you would not get the mark. If you use the words gas, gases, air particles or atmosphere instead of air you would score the mark.

A4 Ice Lollies

Answer

a) Miss Holland's classroom *1 mark*

How to tackle the question

The coldest classroom was the one in which the ice lolly melted slowest. Ice melts faster at warmer temperatures and slower at colder temperatures. You need to look at the bar chart and choose the longest bar: in Miss Holland's classroom it took the greatest number of minutes for the ice lolly to melt. Many children might make the mistake of choosing the smallest bar. This is in fact the classroom that was warmest so the ice lolly melted quickest.

The question asks which classroom was the coldest, it does not ask how long it took for the ice lolly to melt. If you read the time scale from the Miss Holland's classroom bar and write down 65 minutes as your answer, you will not be given any marks. Even though it shows you can read the bar chart, you have not answered the question.

Answer

b) The **higher** the temperature the **quicker** the ice lolly melts.

2 marks

Inside the Science

 This question is about reading graphs and finding patterns in results.

See *Collins Success in Science Book 4,* Chapter 6

How to tackle the question

 This is the same kind of question as question 3b; it is about spotting a pattern. You are asked to describe the pattern or general link between two variables, in this case the temperature of the room and the speed at which the ice lolly melted.

 You could write about the temperature of the room, or the hotter the room, or the colder the room, or the more heat in the room. All these are different ways of describing the varying room temperature.

 There are also different ways to describe how quickly an ice lolly melts. You could write about the ice lolly taking longer to melt or melting more slowly, or it lasting longer.

Once you have decided how to describe the two variables, you need to link them: remember the 'er' rule. You might have written 'because it is hotter it will melt sooner' or 'the colder the room the slower the ice lolly melts'. If you did you would score the 2 marks.

 If you just compare one or two results, for example 'if the room was cold the ice lollies will last longest', you would only get 1 mark.

 Finally, if you try to explain what was happening you would not get a mark because you were asked to describe the link. 'The temperature melts the ice lolly' gets no marks.

Answers and Guidance

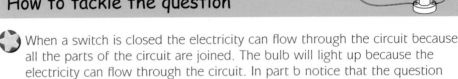

A5 Circuits

Answer

a) the bulb will light (or go on or light up)   *1 mark*

b) the electricity can flow through the circuit (when the switch is closed)   *1 mark*

Inside the Science

These parts of the question are about circuits and switches.

See *Collins Success in Science Book 3*, Chapter 5

How to tackle the question

When a switch is closed the electricity can flow through the circuit because all the parts of the circuit are joined. The bulb will light up because the electricity can flow through the circuit. In part b notice that the question asks you to explain why the bulb lights up when the switch is closed. It is important to say that the circuit is complete and the electricity can flow round. By closing the switch there is no gap in the circuit.

A common mistake children make is to describe what would happen when the switch is closed. For example, if you write, 'because the two sides of the switch touch each other', you will not get the mark because this is not explaining the science. Nor will a simple statement like 'the switch is closed' get you the mark, because you have been told this in the question.

Answer

c)

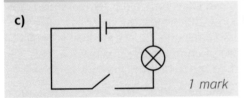

1 mark

Inside the Science

This part of the question is about drawing circuit diagrams.

See *Collins Success in Science Book 3*, Chapter 5

How to tackle the question

To answer this question you need to remember the way to draw a circuit diagram. You do not need to remember the symbols because they are given to you in the question. Make sure there are no gaps around your circuit and that all the wires join up. Some children made the mistake of joining up the symbols incorrectly. Look carefully at the example answer and notice how the symbols are linked by the wires. You get the mark if your circuit has all three components drawn in a circuit. It does not matter what order the components are in.

Only use the symbols given, and check that you draw them correctly in the circuit. The following answers would be wrong and you would not get the mark.

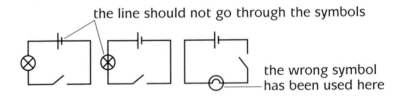

the line should not go through the symbols

the wrong symbol has been used here

Answer

d)

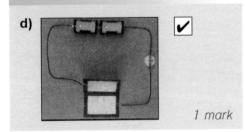

1 mark

How to tackle the question

The positive end of one battery (+) has to be connected to the negative end of another battery (–). You also need to know that two batteries will make the bulb brighter than just one battery, because there is more power in the circuit and passing through the bulb.

Inside the Science

This question is about electricity.

See *Collins Success in Science Book 3*, Chapter 5

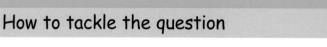

A6 Woodlice

Answer

a) To check their results   *1 mark*

Inside the Science

This part of the question is about being scientific and realising that it is important to try and collect reliable results in an investigation.

See *Collins Success in Science Book 4*, Chapter 6

How to tackle the question

The first thing to notice is that you are told, in the question, that the children carried out a fair test, so you would not get a mark for writing 'to make it fair'. You need to think why you might want to repeat a test three times. Repeating a test gives you more results, so you can spot odd results and check that a similar pattern occurs each time.

A common mistake is to not be precise enough. Answers like 'because we always do things three times in science' or 'three is better than one' will not get the mark because they do not explain why. You have to write about the results and how reliable they are. For example, you could write 'to make sure they were right', or 'to get an average', or 'to see if it was the same each time'.

Answer

b) damp soil and no light (or D)
          1 mark

Inside the Science

This part of the question is about being scientific and making conclusions from results.

See *Collins Success in Science Book 4*, Chapter 6

How to tackle the question

You do not need to know anything about woodlice to answer this question! This question is about looking at the results table and making some conclusions. In all three tests there are more woodlice in section D than in any other section, so the woodlice prefer section D. Look back at the plan of the box and you can see what the conditions were in section D.

Answer

c) under a rotting log   *1 mark*

under a stone   *1 mark*

Inside the Science

This part of the question is about living things in habitats, and the conditions in different places that living things prefer.

See *Collins Success in Science Book 4*, Chapter 1

How to tackle the question

In part b you found out that woodlice prefer dark, damp places. You have to use your experience of the six habitats to select the two places likely to be damp and dark. But even if you have never checked under a rotting log or stone you can rule out some of the other habitats by using your common sense.

Answers and Guidance

Answer

d) leaves ➔ woodlice ➔ shrews

1 mark

Inside the Science

 This part of the question is about food chains and the feeding patterns of living things.

See *Collins Success in Science Book 4*, Chapter 2

How to tackle the question

 To answer this question you need to know how to draw food chains. You are given all the information you need to know about what eats what. All food chains start with a plant or part of a plant, in this case rotting leaves. Remember the arrows always point away from the thing being eaten and towards the eater. You are told that the shrews eat the woodlice but are not told if they are eaten by anything. They must go at the end of the food chain. Finally, you can put woodlice in the middle because they eat leaves and are eaten by shrews.

If you write about other living things or if you do not follow the pattern using the arrows you would lose the marks.

A7 Scales

Answer

a) force (or weight, or pushes/pulls, or the force of gravity)   *1 mark*

How to tackle the question

We measure all forces in newtons. You only have half a line to write your answer so you can be sure that the answer is just one word. So keep it simple and do not take risks. You would not get the mark if you write things like heaviness, mass, grams or the biscuit tin.

Inside the Science

 This part of the question is about forces.

See *Collins Success in Science Book 2*, Chapter 6

Answer

b) 40 (or about 40, or 39 or 41)

1 mark

Inside the Science

 This part of the question is about reading scales, and we have done lots of work on that in the series.

See *Collins Success in Science Book 4*, Chapter 6

How to tackle the question

 You need to read the scale on the scales to answer this question. Remember that the abbreviation for newtons is N, but this has been put in the answer for you. The most common problem with questions like this is not reading the scale correctly but writing down some other unit, such as grams. N has already been printed in the answer so all you need to do is write the number down.

Question A7 continued...

Answer

c) the spring (or the force of the spring, or the table or the reaction force)   *1 mark*

Inside the Science

 This part of the question is about forces and reaction forces in a spring.

See *Collins Success in Science Book 4, Chapters 3 and 4*

How to tackle the question

 You may not have seen a forcemeter like this set of scales but you are given information about how it works at the beginning of the question. The second line of the question states, 'They work because the spring inside is compressed when an object is placed in the pan'. We know that when springs are compressed or squashed they push back against whatever is squashing them. In this case the spring is pushing up against Jason's hand.

Answer

d) 80 N or the same size push as Jason's push   *1 mark*

Inside the Science

 This part of the question is about balanced forces.

See *Collins Success in Science Book 4, Chapter 4*

How to tackle the question

 This question is about balanced forces. Jason pushes against Kerry, who is able to hold the scales still. The scales are not moving so the forces on them must be balanced. Kerry's push must be balancing Jason's push. This means that Kerry's push must be exactly the same as Jason's but in the opposite direction. So the answer is 80 N or 'the same size push as Jason's push'. You are not given the units for this question: it is better not to put any units if you are not sure about them, because you will lose the mark if you write down incorrect units.

A8 Temperature Sensor

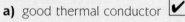

Answer

a) good thermal conductor ✔   *1 mark*

Inside the Science

 This part of the question is about materials and their properties.

See *Collins Success in Science Book 2, Chapter 1*

How to tackle the question

 You need to decide which of the properties of metals is useful when it comes to sensing temperatures. A temperature sensor has to be good at detecting changes in temperature. Metals allow heat to move through them quickly, so this would mean the sensor could pick up changes in the temperature surrounding it. Although metal is magnetic and it is shiny neither of these properties are important for it to be used as a temperature sensor rod.

 You were asked to tick just one box; if you ticked two you would not get the mark.

Answers and Guidance

Answer

b) 17   *1 mark*

Inside the Science

 This part of the question is about measuring temperature and reading scales.

See *Collins Success in Science Book 4*, Chapter 6

How to tackle the question

 You are told that the children first measured the temperature of the room. This is the figure you are trying to get from the graph. On the graph the first temperature (letter A) is the room temperature.

 You might not have seen or used this type of sensor before, but do not worry! You are told on the computer screen that the vertical axis (the axis going up the side) measures 'temperature in °C' so you know that you have to read off against this axis. The scale is quite tricky. There are three jumps from 16°C to 19°C. So each jump is worth 1°C. You are given °C as the units, so remember not to write down a different unit and lose the mark.

Answer

c) B   *1 mark*

d) D   *1 mark*

Inside the Science

 This part of the question is about using a graph to show patterns and trends.

See *Collins Success in Science Book 4*, Chapter 6

How to tackle the question

 To answer parts c and d you need to work out what is happening to the temperature and why. At B on the graph the children had measured the room temperature and then Robert gripped the sensor. Robert was the only thing that touched the sensor, so he was the only thing that could have heated it up. It makes sense then that he grabbed it at B, after which time the temperature started to rise. Remember, you are asked to tick one box, so if you tick two boxes you would lose the mark.

 The words at the start of question b give us the clues. 'Robert gripped the sensor with both hands, held it for a short time and then let it go'. Once Robert let it go, it would start to cool to room temperature. As long as Robert is holding the sensor it will remain as warm as Robert, some way above room temperature. So he lets it go at D and the temperature around the sensor immediately starts to fall.

Answer

e) the temperature dropped or went down (or got colder/smaller or it went down in steps)   *1 mark*

Inside the Science

 This question is about using and interpreting graphs.

See *Collins Success in Science Book 4*, Chapter 6

How to tackle the question

 The clues for this question are on the screen and you do not even need to be able to read the numbers. Look again at the screen and find point D. You will notice that the temperature goes down to point E. It is as simple as that!

 There are two common mistakes that children make with this type of question. The first is to say that the temperature changed without saying that it went down. You have to say which way it changed. The second mistake is to describe what the temperature was at D and at E but not to say what had happened between the two points. For example, the answer 'at D it was 32 and at E it was 27' is accurate but it does not explain that the temperature went down between the two points.

A9 Life Cycle of an Apple Tree

Answer

a)

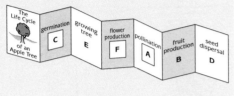

3 marks

How to tackle the question

 You need to think about the life cycle of a flowering plant or tree to answer this question. The easiest place to start is with the growing tree in the ground (E). The blank page before the growing tree page shows that something happens before the tree can grow. This is germination (C). A seed must germinate before the seedling can begin to grow.

There are then two blank pages before the fruit is produced on the plant and eventually the seeds dispersed. If you cross out those stages now on the book, you will have two left, pollination and flower production. Remember, the plant needs to produce flowers before the transfer of pollen can take place so flower production (F) comes before pollination (A).

You get one mark for each box where you have written in the correct letter.

Inside the Science

 This is about the life cycle of the plant.

See *Collins Success in Science Book 3*, Chapter 2

Answer

b) pollen   *1 mark*

Inside the Science

 This question is about pollination.

See *Collins Success in Science Book 3*, Chapter 2

How to tackle the question

 The plants need the insects to crawl into the flower and brush against the stamens which are covered with pollen. The pollen sticks onto the insect and then is transferred to the next flower the insect visits. The pollen sticks onto the stigma of the next flower. This process is called pollination.

 The name of the process 'pollination' would not get the mark because it is not the name of the thing that is carried by the insects between flowers.

Answer

c) The wind can help disperse the seeds from the parent plant (seed dispersal).   *1 mark*

Inside the Science

 This question is about seed dispersal.

See *Collins Success in Science Book 3*, Chapter 2

How to tackle the question

 The wind can help spread the seeds out away from the parent plant. Two common examples are a dandelion seed head being blown by the wind and sycamore 'keys' spinning in the wind.

| Total possible marks for Test A | 40 | Your overall marks for Test A | |

Test B

Skeleton

(a) All humans have skeletons.

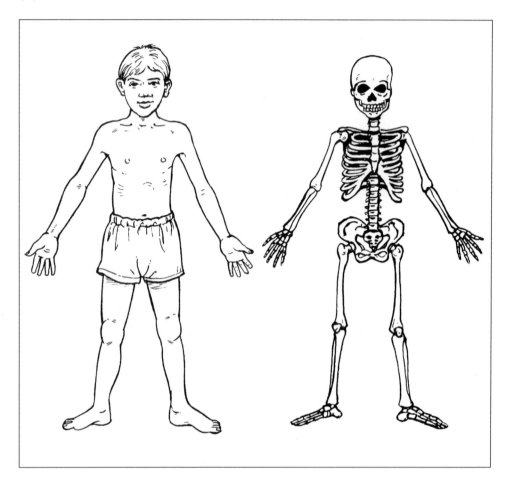

Humans could not manage without their skeleton.

> Write down **TWO** different ways in which the skeleton is
> needed by humans.

(i) ....

....

1 mark

(ii) ....

....

1 mark

2

Solids and Liquids

(a) Ice pops are fruit flavoured drinks which are then frozen inside their plastic wrapper to make a solid ice lolly stick. The plastic wrapper is sealed so the drink cannot leak.

Jade and David wanted to find out how long it took an ice pop to turn back to liquid.

After 55 minutes they saw that the solid ice pop had turned to liquid. They could feel that there was no solid left in the wrapper.

> What is the name of the **process** when a solid turns into a liquid?

✏ ....

1 mark

(b) As Jade and David waited for the ice pop to turn to liquid they noticed drops of liquid forming on the outside of the ice pop wrapper.

> What is the name of this liquid?

Tick **ONE** box.

✏ ice pop ☐   steam ☐   water ☐   juice ☐   mist ☐

1 mark

(c) > What is the name of the **process** which causes this liquid to form on the **outside** of the wrapper?

✏ ....

1 mark

(d)   Where did the liquid on the outside of the ice pop wrapper come from?

....

1 mark

(e)   Jade and David bought some frozen ice pops for a party.

The children thought that there was a good chance that their ice pops might turn into liquid on the way back home. David thought wrapping the ice pops in some layers of newspaper might help.

What would be the effect of the layers of newspaper on the ice pops?

Tick **ONE** box.

The ice pops would:

turn to liquid more quickly ☐

turn to liquid in the same time ☐

turn to liquid more slowly ☐

not turn to liquid at all ☐

1 mark

(f)   It was a hot day. Jade and David measured the temperature outside. It was 25°C.

Draw a line on the thermometer to show the level of the liquid when the temperature is 25°C.

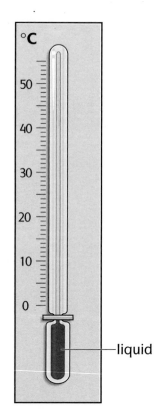

1 mark

3

Shadow

(a) Maria drew a picture of herself and her shadow.

She then found out more about shadows and realised she had made five mistakes.

She put a number next to each mistake on her picture.

The Sun is in front of me ①

My shadow is reflected on the ground ②

③

④

⑤

Mistake number ① was to describe that the Sun was in front of her.

> Where would the Sun have to be to make her shadow in front of her?

✎ ....

....

1 mark

(b) Mistake number ② was to write that the shadow is **reflected**.

> Explain how a shadow is formed.

✎ ....

....

1 mark

Look again at the mistakes labelled 3, 4 and 5.

(c) **Describe what she should have drawn at ③, ④ and ⑤.**

(i)   At 3 she should have drawn ....

....

1 mark

(ii) At 4 she should have drawn ....

....

1 mark

(iii) At 5 she should have drawn ....

....

1 mark

4   **Plants**

(a) Karen and Paul had a competition to see who could grow the biggest sunflower.

To make it fair they used the same kind of sunflower seed from the same packet of seeds.

Karen's sunflower grew taller than Paul's sunflower.

Write **TWO** things which could have caused Karen's sunflower to grow **more** than Paul's sunflower.

(i) Her sunflower had more ....

1 mark

(ii) Her sunflower had more ....

1 mark

(b) The roots of the sunflower plant anchor the plant in the ground.

What other job do the roots do for the sunflower?

✎ ....

1 mark

(c) Karen's sunflower had a lot of large green leaves.

Explain what the leaves do to help the sunflower plant grow well.

✎ ....

....

1 mark

(d) What do all plants need to grow well?

✎ Tick **TWO** boxes.

light ☐   darkness ☐

worms ☐   gravel ☐

pots ☐   nutrients ☐

2 marks

5   **Rocks**

(a) Sally investigated some rocks.

She recorded her observations.

rock	observation		
	can it be scratched with a knife?	does it let water through?	can it be split into flat pieces?
sandstone	yes	yes	no
granite	no	no	no
slate	yes	no	yes
marble	yes	no	no

Look at the table.

Which rock **cannot** be scratched with a knife?

....

1 mark

(b) She sorted **all** the rocks by permeability.

Look at the table.

Write the names of the rocks in each group.

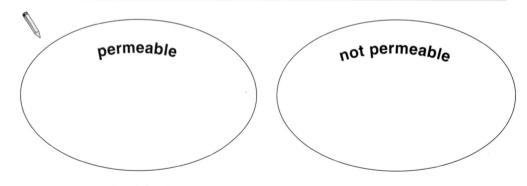

permeable

not permeable

1 mark

(c) Next she sorted them like this.

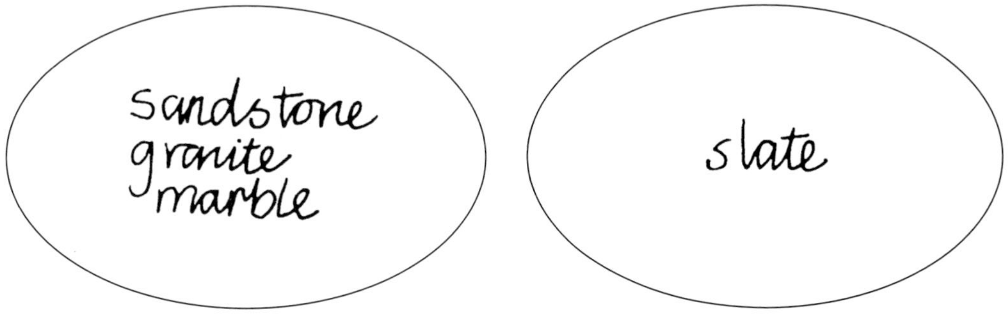

sandstone
granite
marble

slate

Group A   **Group B**

Look at the table.

Describe why the rocks in group **A** make a group.

🖉 ....

1 mark

6   **Measuring Forces**

(a) Saida used a forcemeter to weigh different masses.

She recorded her results as a line graph.

Look at the graph.

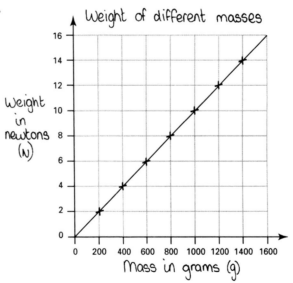

(i)   What mass had a weight of 10 newtons? 🖉 .... g

1 mark

(ii) What weight had a mass of 600 grams? 🖉 .... N

1 mark

(b) Saida then made her own forcemeter using elastic bands.

She used different sized masses to make the scale.

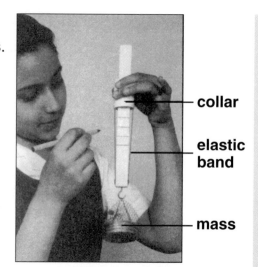

collar

elastic band

mass

What happens to the elastic bands when Saida hangs objects on her forcemeter?

....

....

1 mark

(c) What is it that causes the force of gravity on the objects that Saida is weighing?

....

1 mark

(d) The forecemeter measures the size of pushes and pulls.

Saida used her forcemeter to start a car moving.

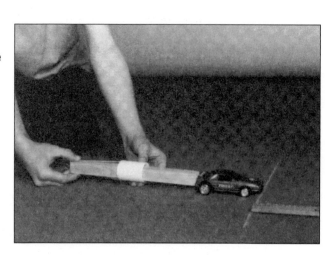

Here is her table of results.

Distance moved by the car using different sized starting forces

Starting force in N	1	2	3	4	5
Distance moved in cm	18	52	140	235	316

> Describe how the size of the starting force affects the distance moved by the car.

✏ ....

....

2 marks

7

Puppies

(a) Sarah's dog, Jessie, has had a litter of 5 puppies.

Sarah keeps a diary to record what happens.

March 2nd
Jessie has had 5 puppies! They are so small, they are about 15cm long and their eyes are tight shut.

March 9th
The puppies are getting bigger and stronger now. Their fur is getting longer too.

March 14th
At last their eyes have opened. The puppies are really strong now. They push each other out of the way to get to their Mum.

March 23rd
The puppies had their first solid food today. They have lots of energy and are great fun to play with.

Look at Sarah's record.

Write down the evidence from the record that shows that the puppies have grown since they were born.

✎ ....

....

1 mark

(b) Tick **THREE** things that all animals do.

✎ play ☐   run ☐

reproduce ☐   grow ☐

give milk to their young ☐   feed ☐

1 mark

1 mark

1 mark

(c) Sarah reads a book to find out more about puppies. The book has an information chart which shows the average mass and length of spaniel puppies when they are born.

The table also shows how these values can change depending on how many puppies are born.

Number of puppies born	Average mass (g)	Average length (cm)
2	280	16
4	250	14
6	210	12
8	190	10

Describe the pattern between the number of puppies born and the mass of each puppy.

✎ ....

....

2 marks

8   **The Earth and Sun**

(a) Anna and David are using a globe as a model of the Earth and a torch as a model of the Sun.

Anna spins the globe to show how the Earth turns on its axis.

How else does the Earth move in space?

....

....

1 mark

(b) How many times should Anna spin the globe to show one day in her model?

Tick **ONE** box.

1	7	21	28	365
☐	☐	☐	☐	☐

1 mark

(c) Anna sticks a model person onto the globe at 3 points, **A**, **B** and **C**. She turns the globe anti-clockwise to show the Earth spinning on its axis.

Anna and David try to work out what time of day it is at each of the positions on the globe.

> When the model Earth is in the position shown in the picture, what times of day are shown at the positions **A**, **B** and **C**?

Choose **ONE** of the words below to complete each sentence.

sunrise **midday** **afternoon**

twilight **dusk** **sunset** **midnight**

One has been done for you.

At **C** it is midday.

At **B** it is ....

At **A** it is ....

1 mark

1 mark

9

Liquids

(a) Nina and Jack were discussing whether all types of tomato sauce were the same.

Jack said, 'All kinds of tomato sauce are made from tomatoes so they must be the same.'

Nina said, 'Well, I think some sauces are thicker than others.'

They decided to investigate to find out who was right.

They bought five types of tomato sauce and put them into five identical bottles. They measured the time it took for the first drop of tomato sauce to fall from the bottle when it was turned upside down.

They recorded their results.

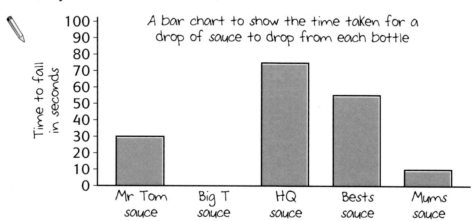

The first drop of Big T sauce took **20 seconds** to drop.

Record this result on the bar chart by drawing a bar to show this length of time.

1 mark

(b) Look at the bar chart.

Which sauce was the thickest?

....

1 mark

Answers and Guidance

Test B

B1 Skeleton

Answer

a) You would get 1 mark for writing about support and 1 mark for writing about movement.

2 marks

Inside the Science

This question is about our skeleton.

See *Collins Success in Science Book 1,* Chapter 1

How to tackle the question

Humans need a skeleton to hold them up, to support them. Without a skeleton we would be all floppy. Be careful not to say we would be like jelly because, although without a skeleton we would be wobbly and floppy, we would not be made of the same stuff as jelly! Answers like 'to help you stand up straight', or 'to keep a solid shape', or 'to stop you being floppy', or even 'without it you can't stand up straight', would get you the mark.

We also need a skeleton to allow us to move. The muscles are attached to the bones and pull against them to make our body parts move. Answers like 'it is needed for movement', 'it helps you run (or any other specific type of movement)', or 'for muscles to pull on', would get you the mark. Answering in the negative, for example 'you can't walk without a skeleton', would also get you the mark.

There are some possible answers to this question that you may not have learnt at school yet. For example, you would get a mark if for part of your answer you wrote that the skeleton protects organs, or that some bones make red blood cells.

A common answer that many children give, although you do not need to learn about this in KS2, is that the skeleton helps protect major organs. For example, the skull protects the brain and the ribs protect the lungs and the heart. You would get a mark if one of your answers was about this.

You were asked for different ways in which a skeleton is important to humans. This means that you have to choose two ways that are very different. The most common mistake in this type of question is to give two answers that are the same, for example two answers about movement or two answers about support.

B2 Solids and Liquids

Answer

a) melting

1 mark

Inside the Science

Changes of state are important and you need to know the names of all of them.

See *Collins Success in Science Book 1,* Chapter 4

How to tackle the question

You are asked about a solid turning to liquid so you have to choose a word that applies to all solids. This process is called melting. You would not get the mark if you wrote about ice thawing or defrosting. Nor would you get the mark if you wrote 'liquefies' or 'turns to a liquid' because a gas also does this when it condenses. Finally, if you write 'changes state' you are not answering the question because you have not given the name of the process.

Answer

b) water

1 mark

How to tackle the question

The liquid is forming on the outside of the ice pop wrapper. The wrapper is sealed so the liquid cannot possibly come from the ice pop. Steam and mist are not the names of liquids even though they are actually made up of water droplets. The only liquid it could possibly be is water.

Question B2 continued...

Answer

c) condensation   *1 mark*

How to tackle the question

 The liquid that we said was water in part b is on the outside of the ice pop wrapper. The question asks for the process that caused this liquid to form. The process is condensation. The wrapper is very cold because it contains the ice pop. When the water vapour in the air surrounding the wrapper touches the cold surface it causes the water vapour to turn back into water droplets.

 You would also get the mark if you wrote 'condensing' or 'condense'.

Answer

d) from the air or atmosphere
                                   1 mark

Inside the Science

Parts b, c and d of this question have been checking to see whether you understand about the condensation of water.

See *Collins Success in Science Book 1*, Chapter 4 for changes of state and *Collins Success in Science Book 2*, Chapter 3 for water in all its forms

How to tackle the question

 Look back at the guidance for part c. We found out that the liquid water droplets on the ice pop wrapper have come from the water vapour in the air. Remember, even though you cannot see it there is water vapour in the air all around us.

 So long as you have indicated that you understand the air outside the wrapper contains water vapour and that is the source of the liquid, you will get the mark. So, 'water vapour' or 'gas' or writing down a correct part of the water cycle, for example moisture in the air, evaporated water or the sea, will get you the mark.

Answer

e) turn to liquid more slowly
                                   1 mark

Inside the Science

This part of the question is about the properties of materials.

See *Collins Success in Science Book 2*, Chapter 1

How to tackle the question

 The layers of newspaper make a good insulator of heat. The layers of paper stop the hot air in the room reaching the cold ice pop. If you slow down the flow of heat to the ice pop, you slow down the speed of melting and the ice pop will turn to liquid more slowly.

Answers and Guidance

Answer

f)

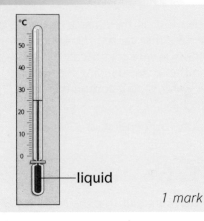

liquid

1 mark

How to tackle the question

⭐ Using equipment and reading the scales of equipment are important skills. To find 25°C on the thermometer you need to find 20°C and then count up the small spaces. On this scale there are ten spaces between 20°C and 30°C so each space is worth one degree. You need to count up five spaces past 20°C to get to 25°C.

⭐ Your line on the thermometer can be between 24 and 26 to get the mark.

Inside the Science

✦ This part of the question is about taking readings from scales.
See *Collins Success in Science Book 4*, Chapter 6

B3 Shadow

Answer

a) behind her   *1 mark*

How to tackle the question

 If you write 'above her head' you are not giving enough information. If the Sun is directly above her head there would be no shadow at all, and if it is above her head and over to one side then the shadow would come out at a different angle. So you have to be clear that the Sun is shining onto her back.

Answer

b) a shadow is made when an object blocks the light.   *1 mark*

How to tackle the question

 A shadow is formed because Maria blocks the light. The light cannot travel through Maria and the shadow is formed behind her. A common mistake is to say the light has to go round Maria. Remember, light travels in straight lines so it cannot go round Maria. If you write about 'light travelling in straight lines' you are giving correct information but you are not answering the question so will not get the mark.

 If you write that 'light cannot get past Maria' you are not answering the question either because lots of light gets past her, it is only the light that hits her back that does not get past.

Answer

c) i) the shadow touching her feet
           1 mark
ii) the arm by her body   *1 mark*
iii) no eyes, nose and mouth
         (shadows do not contain
         any detail)   *1 mark*

How to tackle the question

 The key to part c is to decide what is wrong and then think of words to say what she should have drawn, keeping it as simple as possible. At 3 the shadow feet should have been touching Maria's feet. Shadows always start from the base of the object, in this case Maria's feet!

 If you write 'her legs together' or 'her feet the other way round' then you are not being precise enough. Notice that the answer has been started for you. It is much easier to finish a sentence than start a new one. If you decided to write what was wrong with the drawing rather than what she should have drawn you would still get the mark, but it is a risk. For example, if you write, 'there's a gap between her feet and the shadow' you are starting a new sentence in your answer. Although the person marking your test would want to give you the mark you have made it complicated.

Question B3 continued...

Inside the Science

 This question is about shadows. It is worth learning all about shadows because they come up in the tests year after year.

See *Collins Success in Science Book 1*, Chapter 6

How to tackle the question

 In part ii, the shadow of Maria should match the shape of Maria's outline. If you stand on the playground and wave your arms, your shadow will wave its arms too. Whatever you do your shadow does, so in this case the shadow arm should be by her body like her real arm. If you write 'her arm straight' then you have not given enough information and you would not get the mark. Nor would you get the mark if you write things like 'her arm should be the other way round' or 'her arm is wrong' because you have not given enough information. If you write that her arm should not stick out from her body, then you would get the mark.

 Shadows are patches of darkness with light around them. Because they are patches of darkness they have no detail on them. You do not get faces on shadows.

 Common mistakes in part iii are not being clear enough in your answer. If you write 'a face', 'her head is wrong' or 'her head is tilted' then you are not giving enough information. If you write things like 'there are eyes' or 'she has drawn a mouth' you would get the mark if the marker felt sure that you were starting a new sentence to explain what is wrong with the drawing. If you write that she should have a blank face, you will get the mark.

B4 Plants

Answer

a) You could have written any two of:
- light or sunlight;
- water;
- warmth;
- minerals or nutrients. *2 marks*

Inside the Science

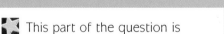 This part of the question is about plants needing water and light to grow.

See *Collins Success in Science Book 3*, Chapter 1

How to tackle the question

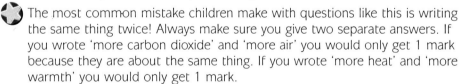

This question is asking about the fact that sunflowers, like other green plants, make their own food using water and the air around them. The energy for making the food comes from light, so this will get you 1 mark. If you wrote down air or named a gas in air, for example carbon dioxide or oxygen, then you would score 1 mark. If you know that the process is called photosynthesis and you wrote that, you would get the mark, as you would if you wrote 'more food was made'. Sun or sunshine would get a mark unless you have already written light or warmth.

 The most common mistake children make with questions like this is writing the same thing twice! Always make sure you give two separate answers. If you wrote 'more carbon dioxide' and 'more air' you would only get 1 mark because they are about the same thing. If you wrote 'more heat' and 'more warmth' you would only get 1 mark.

Another problem is that you have to write enough to convince people that you know the science. For example, if you wrote, 'better soil', what exactly do you mean? If you wrote 'better soil with more nutrients in it' then that would be a good answer to gain a mark, but 'better soil' by itself does not give enough information to get the mark. The same applies to answers like 'better weather', 'more space' or 'being looked after': you must be more precise.

Answers and Guidance

Answer	How to tackle the question

b) The roots take in moisture and nutrients   *1 mark*

⭐ The roots take in water from the soil. They also take in dissolved nutrients in the water. A common mistake is to say that the root takes in food. This is incorrect, a plant makes its own food.

⭐ Make sure you do not repeat information you are told. In the question it says that the roots anchor the plant, so you would not get a mark if you say it holds it in place.

Answer	How to tackle the question

c) the leaves make food or sugar   *1 mark*

⭐ The main job of the leaf is to make food. The leaf takes in light and uses this energy, carbon dioxide from the air and water to make food. Your answer can be kept very simple: the leaves make food for the plant.

Inside the Science

▨ Part b and c of this question are about the jobs that various parts of a plant do.

See Collins Success in Science Book 3, Chapter 1

⭐ There are many other things that a leaf does to help a tree grow well, but the key to this question is to keep it simple and give enough information. For example, if you write things like 'protect the plant' or 'store water' or 'take in water' you are not giving enough information about the use of this in helping the tree grow well. Be careful not to give wrong bits of science. For example, 'they make energy' is incorrect because energy is not made it is just changed from one form to another. 'They help the tree breathe' is incorrect because breathing describes what happens when air is moved in and out of lungs.

⭐ If you write photosynthesis or describe a role that leaves play in photosynthesis and respiration, you will get the mark, but you do not need to know about these processes at KS2.

Answer	How to tackle the question

d) light ✓   *1 mark*

    nutrients ✓   *1 mark*

⭐ Plants need light and nutrients to grow. All the other answers are not essential for the plant to grow. Not <u>all</u> plants grow in pots or have worms or gravel.

Inside the Science

▨ This part of the question is about what a plant needs to be able to grow.

See Collins Success in Science Book 3, Chapter 1

B5 Rocks

Answer	How to tackle the question

a) granite   *1 mark*

⭐ This question is based on rocks that you might not have investigated in school. Do not worry, it is really testing your ability to read an information table. Find the column with the heading 'Can it be scratched with a knife?' Look down the column to find any rocks that cannot be scratched with a knife: it will say 'no'. Read off the name of the rock on the left hand side of the table. Granite is the only rock in the table with 'no' in this column.

Question B5 continued...

Answer

b)

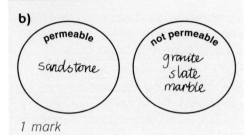

1 mark

How to tackle the question

If a rock is permeable it means that water can pass through it. Find the heading on the table 'does it let water through?' and read off the rocks that say 'yes'. The only rock with 'yes' in this column is sandstone, so it is the only rock that is permeable.

If you are stuck by this question and do not know what permeable means, you should still have a guess! First, look at the other parts of this question on rocks. The first part was about column one, the scratching. So the chances are that this part of the question is going to be about one of the other two columns. If you look at the third part of the question you can work out it is linked to the third column of information. So a good guess would be that that permeability is something to do with letting water through, the second column. This is not a hard and fast rule in test questions, but it is worth doing a bit of detective work if you are stuck with the meaning of some words in a question.

Answer

c) the rocks in group A cannot be split into **flat** pieces   *1 mark*

Inside the Science

This question is about rocks and using tables.

See *Collins Success in Science Book 4*, Chapter 5 to find out about rocks

See *Collins Success in Science Book 4*, Chapter 6 for more information about reading tables

How to tackle the question

Sally has grouped the rocks with the slate on its own and the others together. Look in the columns of the table to find out a grouping like this. Sandstone, granite and marble all have the answer 'no' to the question 'can it be split into flat pieces?' Slate has the answer 'yes' to this question. This fits with the way Sally grouped the rocks: she grouped them according to whether they could be split into flat pieces or not. All the rocks in group A cannot be split into flat pieces.

A common mistake is to write that all the rocks in group A cannot be split into pieces. As *all* rocks can be split into smaller bits, you must say that the rocks in group A cannot be split into *flat* pieces.

B6 Measuring Forces

Answer

a) i) 1000   *1 mark*
   ii) 6   *1 mark*

Inside the Science

This question is about reading from graphs.

See *Collins Success in Science Book 4*, Chapter 6

How to tackle the question

This question is checking to see whether you can read a graph. In part i, find the 10 on the vertical axis (weight in newtons). Follow across until you hit the drawn line and then go straight down and read off the value of the mass. In part ii, you have to work the other way. Find 600 on the horizontal axis (mass in grams), go up until you hit the drawn line and then across to the vertical axis.

Notice that the units for these numbers are given on the page. Do not be tempted to put down another unit. If you get the wrong units you could lose marks. Only put the unit in when it is not given.

Answers and Guidance

Answer

b) They stretch (or extend or get longer/bigger/thinner) *1 mark*

Inside the Science

 This part of the question is about elastic bands and forces.

See *Collins Success in Science Book 2*, Chapter 6

How to tackle the question

 Look carefully at the picture of the forcemeter. The elastic bands are joined onto the collar that Saida is holding and to the moving hook from which the mass is hung. The mass is being pulled down due to gravity and causing the elastic bands to stretch.

 If you wrote, 'they get pulled', you are right but you have not given enough information about what happens to the bands. If you wrote, 'they expand', you would not get the mark because when something expands it increases in volume, it does not necessarily increase in length.

Answer

c) The Earth *1 mark*

Inside the Science

 Check up on gravity: it is a tricky concept but is often in the tests.

See *Collins Success in Science Book 4*, Chapter 3

How to tackle the question

 There is a force of attraction between all things. The bigger the mass of an object the bigger its force of attraction. The Earth is the biggest mass in our world and therefore everything is attracted to the centre of the Earth. This force of attraction is called gravity.

 An answer like 'the mass of the object causes the force of gravity' is also right. This is because there is gravitational force between the mass of the Earth and the mass of the object. You would also get the mark if you wrote the 'mass of the Earth', or 'the mass of the object', or just 'mass'.

Answer

d) The **bigger** the force the **further** the car moves. *2 marks*

Inside the Science

 This part of the question is about forces and about describing patterns in results.

See *Collins Success in Science Book 4*, Chapter 6, for help on questions where you are asked to describe the pattern

See *Collins Success in Science Book 2*, Chapter 6 to find out more about forces

How to tackle the question

 This question asks for a pattern between two factors (variables): in this case the size of the starting force and the distance the car travels. By looking at the data in the table you can see that with a smaller starting force the car did not travel as far and with a bigger starting force the car travelled further.

So did you use the right variables? For ways to describe the starting force, you could choose your words from the following list: bigger force, greater force, harder force, more push. For ways to describe the distance the car travelled you could choose from the following words: more distance, further, longer. Then you need to write a general pattern, for example 'the bigger the push the greater distance it goes'. This answer would get you the 2 marks.

If you just compared one or two results, for example 'the hardest push goes furthest', you would only get 1 mark.

Finally, if you tried to explain what was happening you would not get a mark because you have been asked to describe the link. So, 'the stronger force overcomes friction', would not get any marks.

B7 Puppies

Answer

a) The puppies are getting bigger.
1 mark

How to tackle the question

⭐ 'The puppies play' and 'the puppies can push each other out of the way now' also show that the puppies have grown and would also get a mark.

⭐ This question asks you to use evidence from Sarah's record. This means you need to use something that was written by Sarah. You would not get a mark for other ideas that you may have that are not given in the written record.

Answer

b) Three ticks are needed for 3 marks.

reproduce	✔	*1 mark*
grow	✔	*1 mark*
feed	✔	*1 mark*

How to tackle the question

⭐ Make sure you think about all the different animals – humans along with other creatures such as fish and insects.

Inside the Science

◈ This part of the question is about life processes.
See *Collins Success in Science Book 4*, Chapter 1 for more help with these life processes

Answer

c) The **greater** the number of puppies that are born the **smaller** the mass of each puppy. *2 marks*

Inside the Science

◈ This part of the question is about describing patterns.
See *Collins Success in Science Book 4*, Chapter 6

How to tackle the question

⭐ You are asked to describe a pattern between two things, in this case the number of puppies born in a litter and the mass of each puppy. You need to decide which information in the table to use and then think how to describe the pattern.

⭐ You might have written 'the bigger the litter the lighter each puppy is' or 'the smaller the number of puppies born the heavier each one is' or 'the more puppies that are born the smaller the mass of each one'. Any of these would be fine and would get you 2 marks.

⭐ If you only compared one piece of information, for example, 'when there are only two puppies born they are heaviest', you would only get 1 mark.

⭐ Finally if you tried to explain what was happening you would not get a mark because you were asked to describe the link. So, for example, 'when there are only a few puppies they can grow more easily' would not get any marks.

B8 The Earth and Sun

Answer

a) The Earth moves (or orbits) around the Sun
1 mark

How to tackle the question

⭐ You are told that the Earth spins on its axis so you have to write about another way that the Earth moves in space. The Earth also moves by travelling round the Sun, which it does once every year. The scientific way to say it goes round the Sun is to say the Earth orbits the Sun.

Answers and Guidance

Answer

b) 1 ☑   *1 mark*

How to tackle the question

 The Earth spins on its axis once in a day.

Answer

c) At B it is sunrise   *1 mark*
At A it is midnight   *1 mark*

Inside the Science

This question is about the Earth and Sun.

See Collins Success in Science Book 1, Chapter 5

How to tackle the question

 The key to this question is the direction of the arrow that tells you which way the Earth is moving. Try and imagine you are standing at the point A. It would be dark because the Sun is shining on the other side of the world. It is the middle of the night, midnight. As the Earth spins you slowly come into light. At point B you would just begin to see the Sun. You are coming from darkness or night time, into day time: this part of the day is called sunrise.

 The Earth continues to spin and by point C the Sun would be directly over head. It would appear high in the sky. This happens at midday.

Make sure you use words from the list otherwise you will lose marks.

B9 Liquids

Answer

a)

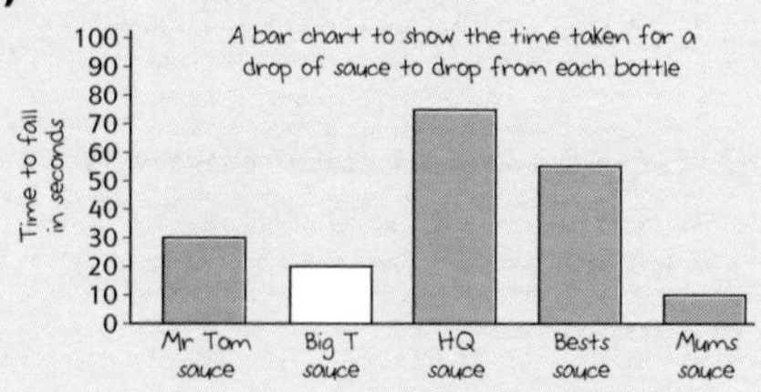

A bar chart to show the time taken for a drop of sauce to drop from each bottle

(bar chart: Time to fall in seconds, vertical axis 0–100; bars for Mr Tom sauce ~30, Big T sauce ~20, HQ sauce ~75, Bests sauce ~55, Mums sauce ~10)

1 mark

How to tackle the question

 Find the space for the Big T sauce bar. Follow across from the 20 seconds mark on the vertical axis (time to fall in seconds) and draw a line across the top of the two squares above 'Big T sauce'.

 You will get the mark so long as the top of your bar is above the right space and touches the 20 second line.

Answer

b) HQ sauce   *1 mark*

Inside the Science

This question is about reading from graphs.

See Collins Success in Science Book 4, Chapter 6

How to tackle the question

When the sauce was thickest it would take the longest time for a drop to fall. So this is the tallest bar on the bar graph, which is HQ sauce.

Total possible marks for Test B | 40 | Your overall marks for Test B | |

48